Written a

GW01563991

Birds of the
Norfolk Broads

Jarrold Colour Publications, Norwich

Introduction

Each summer brings an ever-increasing number of visitors to the Broads. There are many attractions. Not the least is the prospect of spending some time in an environment many parts of which are relatively unspoiled. It is a unique region and particularly so for those interested in natural history. Some will delight in the profusion of plants, others in the variety of insect life, but without doubt the group which captures the imagination of most people is that to which we refer as Broadland Birds. Here is an assemblage which includes such rarities as the marsh-harrier, bittern, and bearded tit and at the same time presents species like the great crested grebe and heron in numbers that can scarce be matched elsewhere. Each bird will be found in particular situations and the visitor who wishes to see them must first consider the main features of the area. Broadland lies in the valleys of the rivers Bure, Yare, and Waveney. These are sluggish streams flowing through a flat alluvial plain which extends inland from Great Yarmouth with spreading arms. Over the years much of the plain has been drained to produce a vast area of grazing marshes. They are intersected by dikes and from these water is transferred to the rivers by a pumping system originally dependent on windmills but now powered by a series of electric pumps. Most of the windmills are derelict.

The broads themselves are artificial having originated as peat cuttings created in medieval times in the upper reaches of the valleys. They are not deep, their basins being about ten to twelve feet below the surrounding land. Flooding of the cuttings probably occurred about the fourteenth century and since that time gradual deposition of organic mud has made them even more shallow.

Because of their origin broads are rarely bounded by firm banks but rather by a curtain of plants such as reeds growing in wet mud and peat. There is a reedswamp in fact, and as the broads become shallower this tends to move outwards and cover the open water. In time the invading blanket of vegetation consolidates, thickens, and is colonised by other plants such as sedge

Open Water

Reedswamp

to create a typical 'fen'. Here one can walk on a quaking mat through a tangle of growth. The consolidation process continues until woody plants like alder can establish themselves to form the typical wet woodland known locally as 'carr'. This progression can be summarised in diagrammatic form as shown below.

It would be very misleading to suggest that all broads are surrounded by such a straightforward pattern of vegetation. There is great variety and each broad has its own individuality. First, they vary in depth and since the reedswamp only invades the open water when mud deposits have raised the floor to within three or four feet of the surface, so the deeper broads will not show any great development of reedswamp, fen, and carr. This is the situation at Ormesby, one of the deepest broads, where the water is for the most part fringed by only a slight screen of reeds. At Barton, a shallow broad, fen development is much more extensive. Then too there are many fens which are cut every two or three years and the reed and sedge removed for thatching. This treatment prevents the establishment of woody plants and the development of carr. In this way great areas of fen are preserved. Those stretching northwards from Martham towards Horsey and across to Hickling are good examples. In other places lack of cutting has allowed extensive carrs to appear until they have reached the very edge of much-reduced broads. Such a situation is well shown if the visitor ascends the tower of Ranworth Church and looks down on those broads lying immediately to the north. The water appears to be ringed by carrs and the landscape should be contrasted with that seen as one sails across Hickling Broad or Horsey Mere, each set in expansive fenland.

In spite of these complexities it is convenient when considering Broadland as a place for birds, to think of it as a patchwork of four main situations. There are the stretches of open water connected by waterways, the reedswamps and adjacent fens, the grazing marshes lying for the most part alongside the waterways and, finally, the carrs. Each situation offers different varieties of food and nesting sites. So each is populated by a distinctive and characteristic group of birds.

Fen   Carr

Open water

It has been mentioned that broads are shallow, rarely exceeding twelve feet in depth. Thus sunlight penetrates the water completely and this factor combined with the presence of good supplies of lime and other mineral salts produces a rich growth of both fixed weed and floating microscopic life. In such luxurious conditions the fish population thrives and the broads offer some of the best coarse fishing in the country. The birds of the open water exploit this abundance of both plant and animal food utilising other parts of the region, such as the reedswamp, for nesting purposes. This is so with some of the best-known species such as great crested grebe, coot, and mute swan. But this does not exhaust the list for there are several species of duck, and others, less prolific, like kingfisher and common tern.

The Great Crested Grebe is a diving bird well equipped to profit from the plentiful supplies of fish and other aquatic life. Obviously the conditions are attractive for nowhere can grebes be seen in greater numbers, about 300 birds being present each year. Almost every broad has its complement. Nevertheless, the distribution is far from uniform. In recent years the greatest numbers have been recorded on Hoveton Great Broad and Blackhorse Broad. Only a few are seen on Horsey Mere where, in the 1970s, they started nesting once again after disturbance by the sea floods in 1938.

Great crested grebes are strangely beautiful birds. Lubbock writing in the last century described them as the greatest ornament of the Norfolk Broads. It is true that when sitting on the water with white neck erect, with head adorned by glistening black ear tufts and chestnut frill, a grebe is a fine ornament but there are several other species which are candidates for the term 'greatest'.

The grebes are not resident but arrive in February or March. Almost immediately they begin their fantastic pre-mating display, a complex performance of head-shaking and neck-stretching accompanied by groans and growls of a most unbird-like nature. By April the first floating nests have been anchored among the previous year's reeds and the eggs are laid. Quite often these early efforts are unsuccessful. The screen of reeds is thin and either fails to hide the nests from marauding carrion crows or provides inadequate protection from the wave-action accompanying spring gales. Fortunately if these first clutches are lost others follow and by the end of May or early June the adults are swimming around carrying curiously striped black and white chicks on their backs. Development is rapid and by late autumn all but a minority of them have dispersed to spend the winter on estuarine or sheltered coastal waters.

The Coot is another bird which builds a floating nest among the reeds. Indeed it is possible to find nests of coot and grebe within a few feet of each other. From this it would appear that the two species mix quite well. This is

Great Crested Grebe (×

Above: *Coot (×⅕).*

surprising for the coot always seems to be an aggressive bird. Disturbed or alarmed in a reed-bed it emits a sharp and truculent 'kik-kowk' and perhaps its best effort is a loud and explosive metallic 'ting'. Yet although a coot has been observed taking a great crested grebe's eggs the fact that grebes are so numerous indicates that no great harm is done.

As with grebes, coots dive for food but whereas grebes pursue fish actively, coots concentrate more on weed. The species also differ in their winter habits for coots flock together at the end of the breeding season and range the Broads in tight packs.

In spring and summer the commonest duck is Mallard. It far outnumbers all others. When breeding starts in March, the drakes, conspicuous with their bottle-green heads and white collars, are often to be found swimming in dikes or sheltered pools within the carrs not far from their sitting mates. By May most clutches have hatched and broods of ducklings are familiar

Top of page: *Drake Mallard (× ⅕).* **Above:** *Greylag Goose (× 1/10).*

sights on rivers or broads. Mallard are surface-feeding ducks and so too are the other species commonly seen, Shoveler and Teal. Drake shovelers are outstanding birds easily recognised by their spoon-like bills which are ideal for dabbling, their white breasts and chestnut flanks. At a distance teal can be distinguished by size for they are the smallest of European ducks. Not so widespread as mallard, shoveler and teal reach their greatest numbers in the vicinity of Ranworth. But although these three are most commonly found, the less common species must also be included. Each year a few Garganey and Gadwall breed in quieter areas along with the occasional pair of Pintail. The only diving ducks normally recorded as nesting are Pochard and Tufted Duck.

A number of pairs of Shelduck rear families around Breydon Water and the species is readily observed feeding on the mud-flats which are uncovered at low water. Geese are represented by feral Greylag, which are most evident at Wroxham and Salhouse, together with the Canada Goose, which often nests in sheltered areas close to the waterways.

Mute Swans feed on submerged vegetation, dipping their long necks under water and even 'up-ending' when necessary. It is difficult to imagine conditions more ideal for them than those offered by the Broads. Food is plentiful and their massive nests can be built among the reeds or on the several small islands which are a feature of some waters. By midsummer, family parties are afloat, the parents accompanying more darkly coloured cygnets. At the end of the year there is a tendency to form flocks and signifi-

Upper left: *Canada Goose* ($\times \frac{1}{10}$). **Left:** *Mute Swans* ($\times \frac{1}{15}$). **Above:** *Kingfisher* ($\times 1$).

cant numbers can be seen on flooded marshland often in company with winter-visiting Bewick's Swans.

   With such good fishing Kingfishers might be expected to be extremely abundant yet surprisingly they do not quite live up to this expectation. From time to time they can be seen flashing across a broad or startling

Top of page: *Swallow (×⅔).* **Above:** *Common Tern (×²⁄₇).*

fishermen by alighting on their rods, but the numbers are by no means great. It is probable that the main reason is lack of suitable breeding sites.

The kingfisher needs steep banks in which to burrow. A typical broad does not provide them and the bird must look to more artificial sites such as disused marlpits or the sides of dikes or 'cuts' where these are sufficiently high. It is in such situations the kingfisher flourishes best.

Over the open water Swallows and Martins swoop and feast on the rich hatches of flies. Flighting alongside, it is often surprising to see black-capped sea swallows or terns. Although usually associated with the coast,

Common Terns prosper around inland waters if they can find suitable places to nest. They readily accept something solid and each year their needs are met by specially constructed rafts at Ranworth and the wooden platform which covers the outlet pipe at Ormesby. In addition the Rush Hills at Hickling are used regularly and occasionally isolated pairs reside on small islands scattered around the Broads.

Similarly, Little Terns can sometimes be seen in June and July fishing those broads adjacent to the coast, hovering and diving to snatch small fish from the water. They have chicks on the pebble-strewn sandy beaches and presumably venture inland when sea-fishing is not productive.

The Black Tern is another species which appears over the open water for very short spells. Regrettably it does not nest around the Broads, but often during the spring migration parties will halt for a few hours to rest and feed. They are most frequently observed in May and are especially abundant when the winds are in the easterly quarter.

Lastly the Black-headed Gull should be mentioned. Birds can be seen about most broads during the summer months. Although there are no massive gulleries at present, smaller colonies exist at such places as How Hill on the River Ant and at Cantley on the River Yare. Groups of a few pairs may settle down from time to time elsewhere.

Black-headed Gull (×⅕).

Reedswamp and Fen

Birds of the reedswamp and fen include the rarest species of Broadland. It is here we find Bearded Tits and Bitterns, Water-Rails and harriers. In addition there are many small birds, warblers and buntings, which like the tits are insectivorous.

The plants of the reedswamp – bulrush, reedmace, and common reed – have the lower parts of their stems in water and act as ladders linking two worlds. So the aquatic nymphs of damsel flies ascend them before their final moult. As they pause to expand and dry their wings they are easy prey. Similarly the ladders allow small birds to descend to the water's surface and snatch swarms of midges as they hatch. Again the plants do not serve solely as feeding-perches but also as food for caterpillars, such as those of the Wainscot moths, and these in turn are consumed by birds.

In contrast to the reedswamp, the fens appear to produce much less insect life. This is especially true if the fen be dominated by saw-sedge, the leaves of which are tough, evergreen, and impregnated with mineral matter. Most insects seem to ignore them. However, the older leaves spread-eagle and the toothed-margins interlock producing a dense cover, difficult to penetrate and ideal for concealing small nests. Thus for many small birds reedswamp and fen are complementary. They nest in the dense, drier fen but keep up a constant procession to and from the reedswamp or wetter parts of the fen, in order to obtain food.

The first of the warblers, the Reed Warbler, confines itself almost entirely to the reedswamp. Its nest is a deep open purse woven round a handful of reeds, the suspended home of a swamp-dweller. Rarely does the bird reach this country before the very end of April or early May and it is probable that the late arrival is timed to coincide with the growth of new reed. But having arrived, it remains concealed, flitting like a gymnast from stem to stem, uttering an apparently endless chattering song. A shy bird, its plumage is not distinctive since it is uniformly brown above and creamy white below with no pronounced features on the head.

The Sedge Warbler is a much bolder bird. Its back is brown, darkly streaked, and the eye is surmounted by a conspicuous creamy white eye stripe. It scolds, 'tuc', and churrs from cover, and when displaying in late April and May rises vertically in the air on fluttering wings, trilling continuously. There is no mistaking when the sedge warblers have arrived.

Our third warbler, the Grasshopper Warbler, is not so abundant as the other two. It is very much a bird of the tangled fen and its presence is recognised not so much from sight as from the song, a long sustained and high-pitched mechanical trill. Hence the local name, the 'reeler'.

Bearded Tits and Reed Buntings complete the population of small birds.

Reed-Warbler (×⅔).

Above: *Sedge Warbler (×1).*

Both are classed as residents but at the end of the summer both show the same tendency to form parties which sometimes break out and roam far afield. In early spring they return to their breeding grounds, but whereas reed buntings are widely distributed, bearded tits show a preference for the fens adjacent to the coast. The area including Horsey Mere, Martham Broad, Heigham Sounds, and Hickling Broad is their great stronghold.

Without doubt bearded tits are the most beautiful of the small birds of the Broads. Rufous-backed and grey-headed, the cocks splashed with a strikingly black moustache, they sweep across the fen with whirring wings and trailing tails. They resemble miniature pheasants and are indeed known as 'reed pheasants'. The bird pictured opposite is a well-marked cock. Hen birds lack the black moustache and although grey-headed are fawn-capped. Both sexes possess a compelling yellow-ringed eye. Their

Above: *Cock Bearded Tit* ($\times \frac{1}{2}$). **Below:** *Cock Reed Bunting* ($\times \frac{3}{5}$).

Above: *Bittern* (×⅕). **Right:** *Water Rail* (×½).

numbers vary considerably from year to year for they are not robust birds
and a hard winter decimates them. But they recover quickly, three broods
in a season being quite usual.

Reed buntings are probably the most conspicuous of the small birds,
well known to all who sail the waterways. The cock has a black cap and
throat with an encircling white collar. He is often seen clinging to the stem
of a swaying reed, raising the feathers of his black cap and forever flicking
and expanding his dark tail. The female is brown-headed with a buff-
coloured eye stripe together with a light moustachial streak. When parent
birds are carrying food for chicks their bills are crammed with caterpillars
for although buntings are seed-eating for most of the year, they rear their
families on an insectivorous diet.

The Bittern disappeared from Broadland as a breeding species in the second half of last century. It returned in 1911 and by mid-century had consolidated its position so that most fens harboured at least one pair. Unfortunately, although still present, its numbers now appear to be somewhat reduced and there is some concern for the future.

A large bird, the bittern is excellently camouflaged for life in a fen. Its legs are green, its body buff mottled and barred with brown so that when it extends and erects its neck in alarm, it tends to melt into the background of reeds. In spring the male proclaims its presence by the unique call, the 'boom'. This is a short series of soft grunts of remarkable carrying power not unlike brief blasts from a distant foghorn at sea. But while the boom is the characteristic call of the cock, the hen too has a voice. On the wing she can emit a sharp 'aark'. In contrast, threading her way through the reeds to the nest, she utters a soft bubbling trill recognised by the chicks, which in appearance display their reptilian ancestry perhaps more than the young of any other species. Most frequently nesting occurs in that part of the fen where the water-level is just, but only just, below the surface. It can be in reed or sedge. Since the main food of the bittern includes small fish, eels, frogs, and aquatic insects, the hen must fly to favoured swamps and grown-up dikes for food. It is then that visitors to the Broads are most likely to see the bird, heron-like in flight but identified by the shades of brown rather than grey and black.

Though it is not uncommon to see the bittern flying, the visitor will be very lucky to catch a glimpse of the Water-Rail. It feeds and breeds in the congested fen and as with the grasshopper-warbler is heard rather than

seen. Fortunately its voice is quite distinctive. It squeals almost in the manner of young pigs quarrelling over food. Local people say the bird is 'sharming'. In the fen the nest is extremely well concealed, generally in one of the wetter regions, and if disturbed the bird slips away and one is aware of a brown shape snaking through the reeds. It is rather smaller and more slender than a moorhen, brown above, slate-blue below, the head distinguished by a long red bill. Very occasionally it can be observed at the water's edge or nervously crossing a Broadland bank from one fen to another.

Three species of harrier are associated with the Broads. The Hen-Harrier is a winter visitor, the Marsh and Montagu's Harriers come in summer. They are predators and they quarter the reedbeds and marshes searching for food, mainly small birds and mammals. With long wings flapping they fly, almost lazily, at no great height, gliding from time to time with wings fixed and forming a wide 'V' above the back. Suddenly they pounce upon some unsuspecting prey. If they are feeding young, the cock does most of the hunting and when successful returns to a point above the nest, calls the female and transfers the prey in mid-air. This 'pass' is a beautiful exhibition of controlled flying, the hen taking the food as the cock releases it from his foot.

As with other rarities harriers have been persecuted over the years by gunners and collectors but due to protection, especially by the Norfolk

Marsh-Harrier male.

Montagu's Harrier male.

Montagu's Harrier female.

Marsh-Harrier female.

Montagu's Harrier (×¼)

Naturalists' Trust at Hickling and Major Anthony Buxton at Horsey, it was possible in mid-century to consider them as regular breeders. Regrettably, however, it must be recorded that in recent years their numbers have declined. No Montagu's harriers have bred since 1957 and although the marsh-harrier has been more persistent latterly it has only nested success-fully on one or two occasions. It is not easy to account for the situation and probably more than one factor is involved.

In the case of Montagu's harrier the disappearance from the Broads has been accompanied by a general diminution in the numbers occurring else-where in Britain, the species being one of the rarest of our nesting birds.

The precarious status of the marsh-harrier is less easily understood in view of the greater success it has achieved in neighbouring Suffolk. Can it be that the bird which is more sensitive to disturbance than most is put off by the ever-increasing volume of traffic along the waterways and broads? The number of craft mounts yearly and there must be some limit to the intrusion of a harrier's world which a bird will tolerate. Or is the reduction in numbers an indirect effect of a fundamental change which has taken place in the general ecology of the Broads which has affected the aquatic life and, at the summit of the food chain, the harriers?

Left: *Common Snipe (×⅓).*
Opposite: *Redshank (×³⁄₇).*

Grazing Marshes

It has been mentioned that the grazing marshes are the products of constant drainage over many years. Intersecting dikes collect and conduct the water to pumps and as the soil has become drier, it has settled until at the present time the marshes lie below the level of the main waterways from which they are separated by banks or walls. There are immense stretches of such reclaimed land and the visitor sees the most striking impression of their magnitude when travelling along the road from Acle to Great Yarmouth which extends for seven miles quite straight and apparently endless. Drained land stretches southwards from the road to the wall enclosing Breydon Water, the estuary which receives the Broadland rivers, while to the north it extends as far as Mautby and Caister. In this single area there are more than fifteen square miles of grazing marshland and this is only a part of the total which lies alongside the different rivers.

The marshes vary very much in quality. The best produce a rich growth of grass and in summer support large numbers of cattle. Others, perhaps not so well drained, have grass interspersed with clumps of rushes, a sign of wetter conditions. Rarely can any marshes be described as dry and the

ground is always capable of exploitation by birds which obtain food from the inhabitants of the soil. Three such species are the Common Snipe, Redshank, and Lapwing.

Common snipe are present at all seasons of the year. They favour the poorer marshes where the ground is soggy and wet. Here they can insert their long beaks with ease while probing for worms and insect larvae. If disturbed, they dart away in zigzag fashion close to the ground, uttering as they go a harsh 'scape-scape'. In winter appreciable numbers can be flushed in this way, but many of these depart in spring, leaving a small population to breed. By March the birds are indulging in their aerial display flights. As they rise to a good height, turn and plunge earthwards with tail spread, the outermost feathers vibrate in the air and produce the tremulous hum which is referred to as 'drumming'. It is one of the special sounds of spring. Four pointed eggs are laid within a grassy tuft or a group of rushes and the striped, tawny chicks are particularly attractive.

Redshanks are summer visitors to the marshes. They arrive in late February and immediately the air is filled with their flute-like pipings. Always restless, they are easily disturbed and when alerted show the typical bobbing action of their tribe. Perhaps the best view to be obtained of a redshank is that of an alarmed bird which, after alighting on a marsh gate, holds its wings vertically for a moment before folding, and then bobs on its red legs, scolding continuously with a clipped 'teuk-teuk-teuk'. For nesting they favour the drier marshes and the eggs are secreted within rank grass which screens them from above. Not so long-beaked as a snipe, the redshank depends more on the contents of the soil near the surface and seems to prefer feeding along the margins of the dikes. Here it can be seen daintily picking its way as it does on the mud-flats of the coast where it spends the rest of the year from August until the following spring.

In addition to the redshank, the drier marshes attract the Lapwing which nests, not within a dense tuft of grass, but in the open and usually upon some slight elevation where the nesting cup or 'scrape' is hollowed out. Flocks of lapwings are a common sight in winter but in spring they break up and pairs establish themselves in favoured situations. While the snipe drums in the heavens, the heavier lapwing with blunt-tipped wings tumbles and twists erratically at lower levels, just missing the ground in its downward sweeps. It screams 'pee-wit' and variations of this cry are uttered not only in flight but also as it rests on the ground with crest erect. Although apparently black and white birds, on closer inspection, lapwings show many subtle shades of metallic green. They are abundant and among the commonest birds of the marshes.

There are small birds too on the marshes and the three most prominent are the Yellow Wagtail, Pied Wagtail, and Skylark. All of them are attracted

Above: *Cock Yellow Wagtail (×⅔).* **Below:** *Pied Wagtail (×⅔).*

by the insect life which they hunt among the grass or by the dikes. Perhaps the yellow wagtail is the species especially associated with the grazing marshes. It is a summer visitor and the buttercup-yellow cocks brighten the scene considerably when they first appear in spring. Yellow wagtails always nest on the ground, and in so doing differ from the pied wagtail which tends to use sheltered situations such as recesses in buildings or reed-stacks, and holes in pollarded willows. The yellow wagtail feeds and breeds on the marshes but the pied is not so specific, hunting gnats and midges by the riverside and, on occasion, taking insects in flight over open water.

Apart from providing a rich supply of worms, snails, and insects, the marshes also have a population of small mammals. Of these the short-tailed field vole is the most abundant but there are others such as shrews and mice. All of them are preyed upon by weasels. In addition they provide the main food of Kestrels and Barn Owls, both present in good numbers.

In the daylight hours a hovering kestrel is one of the most characteristic features of the marshland scene. On quivering pointed wings the bird hangs

Skylark ($\times \frac{1}{3}$).

in the air, tail feathers fanned out and the head, pointing towards the wind, is depressed to allow both eyes to scan the ground for signs of life. Each pair seems to have its own country, each bird its regular beat. When not hunting they have their favourite perches. A certain telegraph pole or isolated bush may be the resting-place of one individual. Similarly, year after year, one pair of birds tends to be faithful to a specific nesting site. It may be a ledge within a deserted windmill, a hole in a tree, or the old nest of a carrion crow. Exceptionally the eggs may be laid on the ground in some marshland cattleshed. They are incubated by the female, a beautiful barred rusty-brown bird which continues to brood the young for the first two weeks of their lives. From time to time the cock brings food to some point close to the nest and calls the female with a rippling high-pitched trill – 'wrreee'. She flies to him and quickly returns to the nest with the prey. It is only when the young are larger that the cock, in the absence of the hen, comes to the nest and shows himself to be a redder bird than his mate with a light grey head and tail which ends in a broad black band. By midsummer the young are flying and for a while the family remains together. No doubt during this period the young are developing their hunting skill before becoming completely independent.

As dusk approaches, the kestrel ceases hunting and retires. Nevertheless the small mammals of the marshes are given no respite for as one hunter

Above: *Cock Kestrel* (×⅓). **Opposite:** *Hen Kestrel* (×⅕).

suspends activities, another takes over. As the sun sets the barn owl sweeps out on noiseless wings, a white ghost-like form beating over the marshes and continually searching for voles in the grass below. There is no hovering but suddenly the owl checks itself in flight and dives to strike some luckless prey. If successful the bird rises, carrying the kill in the left foot whence it is transferred to the beak immediately prior to feeding.

Just as barn owls utilise the same type of food as kestrels, very often similar sites are chosen for nesting. The church-tower or deserted windmill may harbour kestrels or barn owls. Indeed it is not unknown for both species to be housed at the same site within a few feet of each other. At a nesting or roosting point the true beauty of the barn owl can be appreciated. Although in flight the whiteness of the bird is impressive, at close quarters the delicate mottled buff of the back and upper parts of the wings establish it as one of our most striking birds.

Herons can be seen throughout Broadland but it is probably correct to consider them among the birds of the grazing marshes. They exist by fishing, and like fishermen need to stand by the water's edge or wade in the shallows. So the sight of a statuesque Grey Heron by a dike, animated only when it snatches a frog, beetle, or vole from the water, is typical of the marshland. Alternatively, herons haunt the mud-flats of Breydon Water searching for eels and flat-fish but the Broads are too deep for such activities and can only be fished where there is a solid platform adjacent to the water. Hence the major heronries of Broadland are close to Breydon and the extensive associated marshes. Those at Wickhampton, Mautby, and Buckenham are so situated while the great heronry at Ranworth is near to the Bure marshes. If the lower reaches of the Yare and Bure be considered as a single unit, then each year approximately one hundred pairs of herons will be nesting in the area. By midsummer the young are flying to the marshland dikes to feed and during July and August people sailing across Breydon Water are impressed by the numbers fishing in the shallows.

Above: *Barn Owl* (×⅓). **Right:** *Heron* (×⅐).

Left: *Tree Creeper (×1).*
Opposite: *Long tailed Tit (×½).*

Carr

Because of their origin carrs are treacherous and uninviting. To explore them one should be prepared to squelch through dense wet undergrowth and for this reason they are relatively undisturbed. So the carrs constitute a refuge within which several birds associated with the Broads breed unmolested. The great heronries are to be found here and while many kestrels and barn owls nest in marshland buildings, a proportion occupy trees within the carrs. Wild ducks, too, often breed while the Moorhen, though more normally confined to the dikes, builds in the wetter parts.

But none of these birds is solely confined to the carr and there is, in addition, another population similar to that found in more normal woodland. Some hollow trees are used by Tawny Owls, typical woodland owls, and the

Long-eared Owl is also known to nest occasionally. Of the small birds, there are numerous tits and warblers. Again, since carrs are inaccessible, it is not surprising to find there many birds which are persecuted elsewhere. Wood Pigeons and Carrion Crows, Magpies and Jays are good examples together with one or two pairs of Sparrow Hawks.

A special feature of carrs is the high proportion of trees which die at an early age. This seems to be particularly true of alders. Their roots are forever enclosed in waterlogged peaty soil; aeration must be very poor. The trees weaken, they are quickly attacked by fungi and destroyed. So the carrs are full of rotten trunks and stumps which have succumbed in this way. Consequently Tree Creepers are frequent, nesting beneath the flaking bark, but more particularly there are woodpeckers. The Great Spotted Woodpecker is commonest. It searches the rotting timber for boring insects and on occasion descends to explore the mud for grubs. Green Woodpeckers are much more rare, probably because ants, their favourite food, prefer drier terrain. Thus although carrs do not contain the most exciting birds in Broadland nevertheless they offer much of interest.

Above: *Willow Warbler* (×1). **Below:** *Great spotted Woodpecker* (×⅘).